My Summer Reading Journal

Book Title	Author	Started On	Finished On	I liked it (Y/N)

Book Title	Author	Started On	Finished On	I liked it (Y/N)

Date:

Book Title: _____   Number of pages read:

Favorite part: _____
_____
_____

New Word of the day: _____

What the word means: _____
_____

Use it in a sentence: _____
_____

Rate your reading passage today: 😀 😍 🤣 😎 🤔 🙁 😴 😢
□ □ □ □ □ □ □ □

Draw your favorite part:

Date:

Book Title: _____   Number of pages read: _____

Favorite part: _____
_____
_____

New Word of the day: _____

What the Word means: _____
_____

Use it in a sentence: _____
_____

Rate your reading passage today: 😃 😍 🤣 😎 🤔 🙁 😴 😢
☐ ☐ ☐ ☐ ☐ ☐ ☐ ☐

Draw your favorite part:

Date:

Book Title: _____   Number of pages read: _____

Favorite part: _____
_____
_____

New Word of the day: _____

What the word means: _____
_____

Use it in a sentence: _____
_____

Rate your reading passage today: 😃 😍 🤣 😎 🤔 🙁 😴 😢
☐ ☐ ☐ ☐ ☐ ☐ ☐ ☐

Draw your favorite part:

Date:

Book Title: _____ Number of pages read: _____

Favorite part: _____
_____
_____

New Word of the day: _____

What the word means: _____
_____

Use it in a sentence: _____
_____

Rate your reading passage today: 😃 😍 🤣 😎 🤔 🙁 😴 😢
                                  ☐ ☐ ☐ ☐ ☐ ☐ ☐ ☐

Draw your favorite part:

Date:

Book Title: _____ Number of pages read: _____

Favorite part: _____
_____
_____

New Word of the day: _____

What the word means: _____
_____

Use it in a sentence: _____
_____

Rate your reading passage today: 😃 😍 🤣 😎 🤔 🙁 😴 😢
☐ ☐ ☐ ☐ ☐ ☐ ☐ ☐

Draw your favorite part:

Date:

Book Title: _____   Number of pages read: _____

Favorite part: _____
_____
_____

New word of the day: _____

What the word means: _____
_____

Use it in a sentence: _____
_____

Rate your reading passage today: 😃 😍 🤣 😎 🤔 🙁 😴 😢
☐ ☐ ☐ ☐ ☐ ☐ ☐ ☐

Draw your favorite part:

Date:

Book Title: _____   Number of pages read: _____

Favorite part: _____
_____
_____

New word of the day: _____

What the word means: _____
_____

Use it in a sentence: _____
_____

Rate your reading passage today: 😀 😍 🤣 😎 🤔 🙁 😴 😢
                                  ☐ ☐ ☐ ☐ ☐ ☐ ☐ ☐

Draw your favorite part:

[drawing box   ]

Date:

Book Title: _____   Number of pages read: _____

Favorite part: _____
_____
_____

New Word of the day: _____

What the word means: _____
_____

Use it in a sentence: _____
_____

Rate your reading passage today: 😀 😍 🤣 😎 🤔 🙁 😴 😢
                                  ☐ ☐ ☐ ☐ ☐ ☐ ☐ ☐

Draw your favorite part:

Date:

Book Title: _____   Number of pages read: _____

Favorite part: _____
_____
_____

New word of the day: _____

What the word means: _____
_____

Use it in a sentence: _____
_____

Rate your reading passage today: 😃 😍 🤣 😎 🤔 🙁 😴 😢
☐ ☐ ☐ ☐ ☐ ☐ ☐ ☐

Draw your favorite part:

Date:

Book Title: _____   Number of pages read: _____

Favorite part: _____
_____
_____

New word of the day: _____
What the word means: _____
_____

Use it in a sentence: _____
_____

Rate your reading passage today: 😀 😍 🤣 😎 🤔 🙁 😴 😢
☐ ☐ ☐ ☐ ☐ ☐ ☐ ☐

Draw your favorite part:

Date:

Book Title: _____   Number of pages read: _____

Favorite part: _____
_____
_____

New word of the day: _____

What the word means: _____
_____

Use it in a sentence: _____
_____

Rate your reading passage today: 😃 😍 🤣 😎 🤔 🙁 😴 😢
☐ ☐ ☐ ☐ ☐ ☐ ☐ ☐

Draw your favorite part:

Date:

Book Title: _____   Number of pages read: _____

Favorite part: _____
_____
_____

New word of the day: _____

What the word means: _____
_____

Use it in a sentence: _____
_____

Rate your reading passage today: 😃 😍 🤣 😎 🤔 🙁 😴 😢
☐ ☐ ☐ ☐ ☐ ☐ ☐ ☐

Draw your favorite part:

Date:

Book Title: _____ Number of pages read: _____

Favorite part: _____
_____
_____

New Word of the day: _____

What the word means: _____
_____

Use it in a sentence: _____
_____

Rate your reading passage today: 😃 😍 🤣 😎 🤔 🙁 😴 😢
☐ ☐ ☐ ☐ ☐ ☐ ☐ ☐

Draw your favorite part:

Date:

Book Title: _____   Number of pages read: _____

Favorite part: _____
_____
_____

New word of the day: _____

What the word means: _____
_____

Use it in a sentence: _____
_____

Rate your reading passage today: 😃 😍 🤣 😎 🤔 🙁 😴 🥲
☐ ☐ ☐ ☐ ☐ ☐ ☐ ☐

Draw your favorite part:

Date:

Book Title: _____   Number of pages read: _____

Favorite part:
_____
_____

New word of the day: _____

What the word means: _____
_____

Use it in a sentence: _____
_____

Rate your reading passage today: 😃 😍 🤣 😎 🤔 🙁 😴 😢
                                   ☐ ☐ ☐ ☐ ☐ ☐ ☐ ☐

Draw your favorite part:

[ ]

Date:

Book Title: _____   Number of pages read: _____

Favorite part: _____
_____
_____

New word of the day: _____

What the word means: _____
_____

use it in a sentence: _____
_____

Rate your reading passage today: 😃 😍 🤣 😎 🤔 🙁 😴 😢
                                  ☐ ☐ ☐ ☐ ☐ ☐ ☐ ☐

Draw your favorite part:

Date:

Book Title: _____ Number of pages read: _____

Favorite part: _____
_____
_____

New word of the day: _____

What the word means: _____
_____

Use it in a sentence: _____
_____

Rate your reading passage today: 😀 😍 🤣 😎 🤔 🙁 😴 🥺
☐ ☐ ☐ ☐ ☐ ☐ ☐ ☐

Draw your favorite part:

Date:

Book Title: _____ Number of pages read: _____

Favorite part: _____
_____
_____

New Word of the day: _____

What the word means: _____
_____

Use it in a sentence: _____
_____

Rate your reading passage today: 😃 😍 🤣 😎 🤔 🙁 😴 😢
☐ ☐ ☐ ☐ ☐ ☐ ☐ ☐

Draw your favorite part:

Date:

Book Title: _____ Number of pages read: _____

Favorite part: _____
_____
_____

New word of the day: _____

What the word means: _____
_____

Use it in a sentence: _____
_____

Rate your reading passage today: 😀 😍 🤣 😎 🤔 🙁 😴 😢
☐ ☐ ☐ ☐ ☐ ☐ ☐ ☐

Draw your favorite part:

Date:

Book Title: _____   Number of pages read: _____

Favorite part: _____
_____
_____

New Word of the day: _____

What the word means: _____
_____

use it in a Sentence: _____
_____

Rate your reading passage today: 😃 😍 🤣 😎 🤔 🙁 😴 😢
☐ ☐ ☐ ☐ ☐ ☐ ☐ ☐

Draw your favorite part:

Date:

Book Title: _____   Number of pages read: _____

Favorite part: _____
_____
_____

New Word of the day: _____

What the word means: _____
_____

Use it in a sentence: _____
_____

Rate your reading passage today: 😃 😍 🤣 😎 🤔 🙁 😴 😢
                                   ☐ ☐ ☐ ☐ ☐ ☐ ☐ ☐

Draw your favorite part:

┌───┐
│   │
│   │
│   │
│   │
│   │
│   │
│   │
│   │
│   │
└───┘

Date:

Book Title: _____   Number of pages read: _____

Favorite part: _____
_____
_____

New word of the day: _____

What the word means: _____
_____

Use it in a sentence: _____
_____

Rate your reading passage today: 😃 😍 🤣 😎 🤔 🙁 😴 😢
☐   ☐   ☐   ☐   ☐   ☐   ☐   ☐

Draw your favorite part:

Date:

Book Title: _____ Number of pages read: _____

Favorite part: _____
_____
_____

New word of the day: _____

What the word means: _____
_____

Use it in a sentence: _____
_____

Rate your reading passage today: 😀 😍 🤣 😎 🤔 🙁 😴 😢
□ □ □ □ □ □ □ □

Draw your favorite part:

Date:

Book Title: _____   Number of pages read: _____

Favorite part: _____
_____
_____

New word of the day: _____

What the word means: _____
_____

Use it in a sentence: _____
_____

Rate your reading passage today: 😀 😍 🤣 😎 🤔 🙁 😴 😢
☐ ☐ ☐ ☐ ☐ ☐ ☐ ☐

Draw your favorite part:

Date:

Book Title: _____   Number of pages read: _____

Favorite part: _____
_____
_____

New Word of the day: _____

What the word means: _____
_____

Use it in a sentence: _____
_____

Rate your reading passage today: 😃 😍 🤣 😎 🤔 🙁 😴 😢
☐ ☐ ☐ ☐ ☐ ☐ ☐ ☐

Draw your favorite part:

Date:

Book Title: _____   Number of pages read: _____

Favorite part: _____
_____
_____

New Word of the day: _____

What the word means: _____
_____

Use it in a sentence: _____
_____

Rate your reading passage today: 😃 😍 🤣 😎 🤔 🙁 😴 😢
          ☐ ☐ ☐ ☐ ☐ ☐ ☐ ☐

Draw your favorite part:

Date:

Book Title: _____   Number of pages read: _____

Favorite part: _____
_____
_____

New word of the day: _____

What the word means: _____
_____

Use it in a sentence: _____
_____

Rate your reading passage today: 😀 😍 🤣 😎 🤔 🙁 😴 😢
☐ ☐ ☐ ☐ ☐ ☐ ☐ ☐

Draw your favorite part:

Date:

Book Title: _____ Number of pages read: _____

Favorite part: _____
_____
_____

New Word of the day: _____

What the word means: _____
_____

Use it in a sentence: _____
_____

Rate your reading passage today: 😃 😍 🤣 😎 🤔 🙁 😴 😢
☐ ☐ ☐ ☐ ☐ ☐ ☐ ☐

Draw your favorite part:

Date:

Book Title: _____   Number of pages read: _____

Favorite part: _____
_____
_____

New word of the day: _____

What the word means: _____
_____

Use it in a sentence: _____
_____

Rate your reading passage today: 😃 😍 🤣 😎 🤔 🙁 😴 😢
☐ ☐ ☐ ☐ ☐ ☐ ☐ ☐

Draw your favorite part:

Date:

Book Title: _____   Number of pages read: _____

Favorite part: _____
_____
_____

New word of the day: _____

What the word means: _____
_____

Use it in a sentence: _____
_____

Rate your reading passage today: 😃 😍 🤣 😎 🤔 🙁 😴 😢
☐ ☐ ☐ ☐ ☐ ☐ ☐ ☐

Draw your favorite part:

Date:

Book Title: _____   Number of pages read: _____

Favorite part: _____

_____

_____

New word of the day: _____

What the word means: _____

_____

Use it in a sentence: _____

_____

Rate your reading passage today: 😃 😍 🤪 😎 🤔 🙁 😴 😢
☐ ☐ ☐ ☐ ☐ ☐ ☐ ☐

Draw your favorite part:

Date:

Book Title: _____   Number of pages read: _____

Favorite part: _____
_____
_____

New Word of the day: _____

What the word means: _____
_____

Use it in a sentence: _____
_____

Rate your reading passage today: 😀 😍 🤣 😎 🤔 🙁 😴 😢
☐ ☐ ☐ ☐ ☐ ☐ ☐ ☐

Draw your favorite part:

Date:

Book Title: _____   Number of pages read: _____

Favorite part: _____
_____
_____

New word of the day: _____

What the word means: _____
_____

Use it in a sentence: _____
_____

Rate your reading passage today: 😃 😍 🤣 😎 🤔 🙁 😴 🥲
☐ ☐ ☐ ☐ ☐ ☐ ☐ ☐

Draw your favorite part:

Date:

Book Title: _____   Number of pages read: _____

Favorite part: _____
_____
_____

New word of the day: _____

What the word means: _____
_____

Use it in a sentence: _____
_____

Rate your reading passage today: 😃 😍 🤣 😎 🤔 🙁 😴 🥹
  ☐ ☐ ☐ ☐ ☐ ☐ ☐ ☐

Draw your favorite part:

Date:

Book Title: _____   Number of pages read: _____

Favorite part: _____
_____
_____

New Word of the day: _____

What the word means: _____
_____

Use it in a sentence: _____
_____

Rate your reading passage today: 😃 😍 🤣 😎 🤔 🙁 😴 😢
☐ ☐ ☐ ☐ ☐ ☐ ☐ ☐

Draw your favorite part:

Date:

Book Title: _____   Number of pages read: _____

Favorite part: _____
_____
_____

New Word of the day: _____

What the word means: _____
_____

Use it in a sentence: _____
_____

Rate your reading passage today: 😃 😍 🤣 😎 🤔 🙁 😴 😢
☐ ☐ ☐ ☐ ☐ ☐ ☐ ☐

Draw your favorite part:

Date:

Book Title: _____   Number of pages read: _____

Favorite part: _____
_____
_____

New word of the day: _____

What the word means: _____
_____

Use it in a sentence: _____
_____

Rate your reading passage today: 😃 😍 🤣 😎 🤔 🙁 😴 😢
☐ ☐ ☐ ☐ ☐ ☐ ☐ ☐

Draw your favorite part:

Date:

Book Title: _____   Number of pages read: _____

Favorite part: _____
_____
_____

New word of the day: _____

What the word means: _____
_____

Use it in a sentence: _____
_____

Rate your reading passage today: 😀 😍 🤣 😎 🤔 🙁 😴 😢
☐ ☐ ☐ ☐ ☐ ☐ ☐ ☐

Draw your favorite part:

┌───┐
│   │
│   │
│   │
│   │
│   │
│   │
│   │
│   │
│   │
│   │
└───┘

Date:

Book Title: _____   Number of pages read: _____

Favorite part: _____
_____
_____

New Word of the day: _____

What the word means: _____
_____

Use it in a sentence: _____
_____

Rate your reading passage today: 😀 😍 🤣 😎 🤔 🙁 😴 😢
☐ ☐ ☐ ☐ ☐ ☐ ☐ ☐

Draw your favorite part:

Date:

Book Title: _____   Number of pages read: _____

Favorite part: _____
_____
_____

New word of the day: _____

What the word means: _____
_____

Use it in a sentence: _____
_____

Rate your reading passage today: 😃 😍 🤣 😎 🤔 😐 😴 😢
☐ ☐ ☐ ☐ ☐ ☐ ☐ ☐

Draw your favorite part:

Date:

Book Title: _____ Number of pages read: _____

Favorite part: _____
_____
_____

New Word of the day: _____

What the word means: _____
_____

Use it in a sentence: _____
_____

Rate your reading passage today: 😀 😍 🤣 😎 🤔 🙁 😴 😢
☐ ☐ ☐ ☐ ☐ ☐ ☐ ☐

Draw your favorite part:

Date:

Book Title: _____   Number of pages read: _____

Favorite part: _____
_____
_____

New Word of the day: _____

What the word means: _____
_____

Use it in a sentence: _____
_____

Rate your reading passage today: 😀 😍 🤣 😎 🤔 🙁 😴 😢
☐ ☐ ☐ ☐ ☐ ☐ ☐ ☐

Draw your favorite part:

Date:

Book Title: _____   Number of pages read: _____

Favorite part: _____
_____
_____

New Word of the day: _____

What the word means: _____
_____

Use it in a sentence: _____
_____

Rate your reading passage today: 😃 😍 🤣 😎 🤔 🙁 😴 🥺
☐ ☐ ☐ ☐ ☐ ☐ ☐ ☐

Draw your favorite part:

Date:

Book Title: _____ Number of pages read: _____

Favorite part: _____
_____
_____

New Word of the day: _____

What the Word means: _____
_____

Use it in a Sentence: _____
_____

Rate your reading passage today: 😃 😍 🤣 😎 🤔 😕 😴 😢
☐ ☐ ☐ ☐ ☐ ☐ ☐ ☐

Draw your favorite part:

Date:

Book Title: _____   Number of pages read: _____

Favorite part: _____
_____
_____

New Word of the day: _____

What the word means: _____
_____

Use it in a sentence: _____
_____

Rate your reading passage today: 😃 😍 🤣 😎 🤔 🙁 😴 😢
☐ ☐ ☐ ☐ ☐ ☐ ☐ ☐

Draw your favorite part:

┌─────────────────────────────────────┐
│   │
│   │
│   │
│   │
│   │
│   │
│   │
│   │
│   │
└─────────────────────────────────────┘

Date:

Book Title: _____   Number of pages read:

Favorite part: _____
_____
_____

New word of the day: _____

What the word means: _____
_____

Use it in a sentence: _____
_____

Rate your reading passage today: 😃 😍 🤣 😎 🤔 🙁 😴 😢
                                    ☐   ☐   ☐   ☐   ☐   ☐   ☐   ☐

Draw your favorite part:

Date:

Book Title: _____   Number of pages read: _____

Favorite part: _____
_____
_____

New word of the day: _____

What the word means: _____
_____

Use it in a sentence: _____
_____

Rate your reading passage today: 😀 😍 🤣 😎 🤔 🙁 😴 😢
☐ ☐ ☐ ☐ ☐ ☐ ☐ ☐

Draw your favorite part:

[   ]

Date:

Book Title: _____ Number of pages read: _____

Favorite part: _____
_____
_____

New Word of the day: _____

What the word means: _____
_____

Use it in a sentence: _____
_____

Rate your reading passage today: 😃 😍 🤣 😎 🤔 😕 😴 😢
☐ ☐ ☐ ☐ ☐ ☐ ☐ ☐

Draw your favorite part:

Date:

Book Title: _____   Number of pages read: _____

Favorite part: _____
_____
_____

New Word of the day: _____

What the word means: _____
_____

Use it in a sentence: _____
_____

Rate your reading passage today: 😃 😍 🤣 😎 🤔 🙁 😴 😢
☐ ☐ ☐ ☐ ☐ ☐ ☐ ☐

Draw your favorite part:

┌─────────────────────────────────────┐
│   │
│   │
│   │
│   │
│   │
│   │
│   │
│   │
│   │
│   │
└─────────────────────────────────────┘

Date:

Book Title: _____   Number of pages read: _____

Favorite part: _____
_____
_____

New Word of the day: _____

What the word means: _____
_____

Use it in a sentence: _____
_____

Rate your reading passage today: 😃 😍 🤣 😎 🤔 😕 😴 😢
☐ ☐ ☐ ☐ ☐ ☐ ☐ ☐

Draw your favorite part:

Date:

Book Title: _____ Number of pages read: _____

Favorite part: _____
_____
_____

New word of the day: _____

What the word means: _____
_____

Use it in a sentence: _____
_____

Rate your reading passage today: 😃 😍 🤣 😎 🤔 ☹️ 😴 😢
☐ ☐ ☐ ☐ ☐ ☐ ☐ ☐

Draw your favorite part:

Date:

Book Title: _____   Number of pages read: _____

Favorite part: _____
_____
_____

New word of the day: _____

What the word means: _____
_____

Use it in a sentence: _____
_____

Rate your reading passage today: 😃 😍 🤣 😎 🤔 😐 😴 😢
☐ ☐ ☐ ☐ ☐ ☐ ☐ ☐

Draw your favorite part:

Date:

Book Title: _____

Number of pages read: _____

Favorite part: _____
_____
_____

New Word of the day: _____

What the word means: _____
_____

Use it in a sentence: _____
_____

Rate your reading passage today: 😃 😍 😝 😎 🤔 🙁 😴 😢
☐ ☐ ☐ ☐ ☐ ☐ ☐ ☐

Draw your favorite part:

Date:

Book Title: _____   Number of pages read: _____

Favorite part: _____
_____
_____

New word of the day: _____

What the word means: _____
_____

Use it in a sentence: _____
_____

Rate your reading passage today: 😃 😍 🤣 😎 🤔 🙁 😴 😢
☐ ☐ ☐ ☐ ☐ ☐ ☐ ☐

Draw your favorite part:

Date:

Book Title: _____   Number of pages read: _____

Favorite part: _____
_____
_____

New word of the day: _____

What the word means: _____
_____

Use it in a sentence: _____
_____

Rate your reading passage today: 😀 😍 🤣 😎 🤔 🙁 😴 🥲
☐ ☐ ☐ ☐ ☐ ☐ ☐ ☐

Draw your favorite part:

Date:

Book Title: _____ Number of pages read: _____

Favorite part: _____
_____
_____

New word of the day: _____

What the word means: _____
_____

Use it in a sentence: _____
_____

Rate your reading passage today: 😃 😍 🤣 😎 🤔 🙁 😴 😢
☐ ☐ ☐ ☐ ☐ ☐ ☐ ☐

Draw your favorite part:

Date:

Book Title: _____ Number of pages read: _____

Favorite part: _____
_____
_____

New word of the day: _____

What the word means: _____
_____

Use it in a sentence: _____
_____

Rate your reading passage today: 😀 😍 🤣 😎 🤔 😕 😴 😢
☐ ☐ ☐ ☐ ☐ ☐ ☐ ☐

Draw your favorite part:

Date:

Book Title: _____   Number of pages read: _____

Favorite part: _____
_____
_____

New word of the day: _____

What the word means: _____
_____

Use it in a sentence: _____
_____

Rate your reading passage today: 😀 😍 🤣 😎 🤔 🙁 😴 😢
☐ ☐ ☐ ☐ ☐ ☐ ☐ ☐

Draw your favorite part:

Date:

Book Title: _____   Number of pages read: _____

Favorite part: _____
_____
_____

New word of the day: _____

What the word means: _____
_____

use it in a sentence: _____
_____

Rate your reading passage today: 😃 😍 🤣 😎 🤔 🙁 😴 😢
☐ ☐ ☐ ☐ ☐ ☐ ☐ ☐

Draw your favorite part:

Date:

Book Title: _____ Number of pages read: _____

Favorite part: _____
_____
_____

New word of the day: _____

What the word means: _____
_____

Use it in a sentence: _____
_____

Rate your reading passage today: 😃 😍 🤣 😎 🤔 😕 😴 😢
☐ ☐ ☐ ☐ ☐ ☐ ☐ ☐

Draw your favorite part:

Book Title: _____   Number of pages read: _____

Favorite part: _____

_____

_____

New word of the day: _____

What the word means: _____

_____

Use it in a sentence: _____

_____

Rate your reading passage today: 😃 😍 🤣 😎 🤔 🙁 😴 😢
☐ ☐ ☐ ☐ ☐ ☐ ☐ ☐

Draw your favorite part:

Date:

Book Title: _____   Number of pages read: _____

Favorite part: _____

_____

_____

New word of the day: _____

What the word means: _____

_____

Use it in a sentence: _____

_____

Rate your reading passage today: 😃 😍 🤣 😎 🤔 🙁 😴 😢
                                   ☐   ☐   ☐   ☐   ☐   ☐   ☐   ☐

Draw your favorite part:

Date:

Book Title: _____ Number of pages read: _____

Favorite part: _____
_____
_____

New word of the day: _____

What the word means: _____
_____

Use it in a sentence: _____
_____

Rate your reading passage today: 😃 😍 🤣 😎 🤔 🙁 😴 😢
☐ ☐ ☐ ☐ ☐ ☐ ☐ ☐

Draw your favorite part:

Date:

Book Title: _____ Number of pages read: _____

Favorite part: _____
_____
_____

New word of the day: _____

What the word means: _____
_____

use it in a sentence: _____
_____

Rate your reading passage today: 😀 😍 🤣 😎 🤔 🙁 😴 🥺
☐ ☐ ☐ ☐ ☐ ☐ ☐ ☐

Draw your favorite part:

Date:

Book Title: _____   Number of pages read: _____

Favorite part: _____
_____
_____

New word of the day: _____

What the word means: _____
_____

Use it in a sentence: _____
_____

Rate your reading passage today: 😃 😍 😂 😎 🤔 😐 😴 🥺
☐ ☐ ☐ ☐ ☐ ☐ ☐ ☐

Draw your favorite part:

Date:

Book Title: _____   Number of pages read: _____

Favorite part: _____
_____
_____

New word of the day: _____

What the word means: _____
_____

Use it in a sentence: _____
_____

Rate your reading passage today: 😀 😍 🤣 😎 🤔 🙁 😴 😢
☐ ☐ ☐ ☐ ☐ ☐ ☐ ☐

Draw your favorite part:

Date:

Book Title: _____ Number of pages read: _____

Favorite part: _____
_____
_____

New word of the day: _____

What the word means: _____
_____

Use it in a sentence: _____
_____

Rate your reading passage today: 😀 😍 🤣 😎 🤔 🙁 😴 😢
☐ ☐ ☐ ☐ ☐ ☐ ☐ ☐

Draw your favorite part:

Date:

Book Title: _____ Number of pages read: _____

Favorite part: _____
_____
_____

New Word of the day: _____

What the word means: _____
_____

Use it in a sentence: _____
_____

Rate your reading passage today: 😃 😍 🤣 😎 🤔 😕 😴 😢
☐ ☐ ☐ ☐ ☐ ☐ ☐ ☐

Draw your favorite part:

Date:

Book Title: _____   Number of pages read: _____

Favorite part: _____
_____
_____

New Word of the day: _____

What the word means: _____
_____

Use it in a sentence: _____
_____

Rate your reading passage today: 😃 😍 🤣 😎 🤔 🙁 😴 😢
                                   ☐ ☐ ☐ ☐ ☐ ☐ ☐ ☐

Draw your favorite part:

Date:

Book Title: _____   Number of pages read: _____

Favorite part: _____
_____
_____

New word of the day: _____

What the word means: _____
_____

Use it in a sentence: _____
_____

Rate your reading passage today: 😀 😍 🤣 😎 🤔 🙁 😴 😢
   ☐ ☐ ☐ ☐ ☐ ☐ ☐ ☐

Draw your favorite part:

Date:

Book Title: _____   Number of pages read: _____

Favorite part: _____
_____
_____

New word of the day: _____

What the word means: _____
_____

use it in a sentence: _____
_____

Rate your reading passage today: 😃 😍 🤣 😎 🤔 🙁 😴 😢
                                    ☐ ☐ ☐ ☐ ☐ ☐ ☐ ☐

Draw your favorite part:

Date:

Book Title: _____   Number of pages read: _____

Favorite part: _____
_____
_____

New Word of the day: _____

What the word means: _____
_____

Use it in a sentence: _____
_____

Rate your reading passage today: 😀 😍 🤣 😎 🤔 🙁 😴 😢
☐ ☐ ☐ ☐ ☐ ☐ ☐ ☐

Draw your favorite part:

Date:

Book Title: _____   Number of pages read: _____

Favorite part: _____
_____
_____

New Word of the day: _____

What the word means: _____
_____

Use it in a sentence: _____
_____

Rate your reading passage today: 😃 😍 🤣 😎 🤔 😐 😴 😢
☐ ☐ ☐ ☐ ☐ ☐ ☐ ☐

Draw your favorite part:

Date:

Book Title: _____ Number of pages read: _____

Favorite part: _____
_____
_____

New word of the day: _____

What the word means: _____
_____

Use it in a sentence: _____
_____

Rate your reading passage today: 😃 😍 🤣 😎 🤔 😕 😴 😢
☐ ☐ ☐ ☐ ☐ ☐ ☐ ☐

Draw your favorite part:

Date:

Book Title: _____ Number of pages read: _____

Favorite part: _____

_____

_____

New Word of the day: _____

What the word means: _____

_____

Use it in a sentence: _____

_____

Rate your reading passage today: 😃 😍 🤣 😎 🤔 🙁 😴 😢
☐ ☐ ☐ ☐ ☐ ☐ ☐ ☐

Draw your favorite part:

Date:

Book Title: _____ Number of pages read: _____

Favorite part: _____
_____
_____

New word of the day: _____

What the word means: _____
_____

Use it in a sentence: _____
_____

Rate your reading passage today: 😃 😍 🤣 😎 🤔 😐 😴 😢
☐ ☐ ☐ ☐ ☐ ☐ ☐ ☐

Draw your favorite part:

Date:

Book Title: _____   Number of pages read: _____

Favorite part: _____
_____
_____

New Word of the day: _____

What the word means: _____
_____

Use it in a sentence: _____
_____

Rate your reading passage today: 😃 😍 🤣 😎 🤔 😐 😴 😢
☐ ☐ ☐ ☐ ☐ ☐ ☐ ☐

Draw your favorite part:

Date:

Book Title: _____   Number of pages read: _____

Favorite part: _____
_____
_____

New word of the day: _____

What the word means: _____
_____

Use it in a sentence: _____
_____

Rate your reading passage today: 😃 😍 🤣 😎 🤔 🙁 😴 😢
                                 ☐ ☐ ☐ ☐ ☐ ☐ ☐ ☐

Draw your favorite part:

Date:

Book Title: _____ Number of pages read: _____

Favorite part: _____
_____
_____

New word of the day: _____

What the word means: _____
_____

Use it in a sentence: _____
_____

Rate your reading passage today: 😃 😍 🤣 😎 🤔 🙁 😴 😢
☐ ☐ ☐ ☐ ☐ ☐ ☐ ☐

Draw your favorite part:

Date:

Book Title: _____   Number of pages read:

Favorite part: _____
_____
_____

New Word of the day: _____

What the word means: _____
_____

Use it in a sentence: _____
_____

Rate your reading passage today: 😃 😍 🤣 😎 🤔 😐 😴 😢
☐ ☐ ☐ ☐ ☐ ☐ ☐ ☐

Draw your favorite part:

Date:

Book Title: _____   Number of pages read: _____

Favorite part: _____
_____
_____

New word of the day: _____

What the word means: _____
_____

use it in a sentence: _____
_____

Rate your reading passage today: 😀 😍 🤣 😎 🤔 🙁 😴 😢
☐ ☐ ☐ ☐ ☐ ☐ ☐ ☐

Draw your favorite part:

Date:

Book Title: _____   Number of pages read: _____

Favorite part: _____
....
....

New word of the day: _____

What the word means: _____
....

use it in a Sentence: _____
....

Rate your reading passage today: 😃 😍 🤣 😎 🤔 🙁 😴 😢
                                   ☐ ☐ ☐ ☐ ☐ ☐ ☐ ☐

Draw your favorite part:

┌───┐
│   │
│   │
│   │
│   │
│   │
│   │
│   │
│   │
│   │
│   │
│   │
└───┘

Date:

Book Title: _____ Number of pages read: _____

Favorite part: _____
_____
_____

New word of the day: _____

What the word means: _____
_____

Use it in a sentence: _____
_____

Rate your reading passage today: 😃 😍 🤣 😎 🤔 🙁 😴 😢
☐ ☐ ☐ ☐ ☐ ☐ ☐ ☐

Draw your favorite part:

Date:

Book Title: _____   Number of pages read: _____

Favorite part: _____
_____
_____

New word of the day: _____

What the word means: _____
_____

Use it in a sentence: _____
_____

Rate your reading passage today: 😃 😍 🤣 😎 🤔 😐 😴 😢
□ □ □ □ □ □ □ □

Draw your favorite part:

Date:

Book Title: _____ Number of pages read: _____

Favorite part: _____
_____
_____

New word of the day: _____

What the word means: _____
_____

Use it in a sentence: _____
_____

Rate your reading passage today: 😀 😍 🤣 😎 🤔 😕 😴 😢
☐ ☐ ☐ ☐ ☐ ☐ ☐ ☐

Draw your favorite part:

Date:

Book Title: _____   Number of pages read:

Favorite part: _____
_____
_____

New Word of the day: _____

What the word means: _____
_____

use it in a sentence: _____
_____

Rate your reading passage today: 😃 😍 🤣 😎 🤔 🙁 😴 😢
☐ ☐ ☐ ☐ ☐ ☐ ☐ ☐

Draw your favorite part:

Date:

Book Title: _____   Number of pages read: _____

Favorite part: _____
_____
_____

New word of the day: _____

What the word means: _____
_____

Use it in a sentence: _____
_____

Rate your reading passage today: 😀 😍 🤣 😎 🤔 🙁 😴 😢
☐ ☐ ☐ ☐ ☐ ☐ ☐ ☐

Draw your favorite part:

Date:

Book Title: _____   Number of pages read:

Favorite part: _____
_____
_____

New word of the day: _____

What the word means: _____
_____

Use it in a sentence: _____
_____

Rate your reading passage today: 😃 😍 🤣 😎 🤔 🙁 😴 😢
                                    ☐ ☐ ☐ ☐ ☐ ☐ ☐ ☐

Draw your favorite part:

Date:

Book Title: _____ Number of pages read: _____

Favorite part: _____
_____
_____

New Word of the day: _____

What the word means: _____
_____

Use it in a sentence: _____
_____

Rate your reading passage today: 😀 😍 😋 😎 🤔 🙁 😴 🥲
☐ ☐ ☐ ☐ ☐ ☐ ☐ ☐

Draw your favorite part:

Date:

Book Title: _____ Number of pages read: _____

Favorite part: _____

_____

_____

New Word of the day: _____

What the word means: _____

_____

Use it in a sentence: _____

_____

Rate your reading passage today: 😃 😍 🤣 😎 🤔 😕 😴 🥺
⬜ ⬜ ⬜ ⬜ ⬜ ⬜ ⬜ ⬜

Draw your favorite part:

Made in the USA
Monee, IL
28 June 2021